8 CHA
ON PER

&

ANGELS' SONG
WALTER HILTON

TRANSLATED INTO MODERN ENGLISH BY
ROSEMARY DORWARD

SLG PRESS
Convent of the Incarnation
Fairacres Oxford

ISBN 0 7283 0096 6

ISSN 0307-1405

TRANSLATOR'S PREFACE

Walter Hilton died on the vigil of the feast of the Annunciation in 1395/6. Little is known of his career: he probably had connections with Cambridge and may have tried and rejected the solitary life before becoming an Augustinian Canon at the Priory of Thurgarton in Nottinghamshire. His major work is *The Scale of Perfection*, a spiritual guide of great wisdom and charm, which before the Reformation was widely copied and read both in England and on the Continent, but he also wrote *Mixed Life* and other short treatises.

Eight Chapters on Perfection has been found in twelve manuscripts, five of which are incomplete. The present translation is based on MS Petyt 524 in the Library of the Inner Temple, London, edited by the late Professor Fumio Kuriyagawa for the English Literary Society of Japan (*Studies in English Literature*, English Number, 1971) and reprinted in 1980 under the direction of Professor Toshiyuki Takamiya. I am very grateful to Mrs F. Kuriyagawa and Professor Takamiya for their kind permission to use this text.

Walter Hilton's tract is itself translated from the Latin original of Dom Lluis de Fontibus, an Aragonese friar known to have been at Cambridge in 1383 (A. B. Emden, *A Bibliographical Register of the University of Cambridge to 1500*, Cambridge, 1963, p. 236, cited by Professor Kuriyagawa, op. cit. p. 33). Nobody has yet found this book, so we cannot tell what proportion of it Hilton translated or be sure whether his eight chapters represent consecutive chapters of the Latin: his abrupt transition from the somewhat detached tone of the first chapter to the intimacy of the next suggests that they do not, and indeed we are told only the first of the signs of love with its operations before he passes on to the withdrawal of devotion in chapter two, an apparently unrelated topic. The loosely constructed pattern of the later chapters is easier to accept as authorial, though chapter eight gives a curious repetition—apparently a reworking in greater detail—of the last part of chapter five. Both these chapters on the dangers of spiritual love seem to have appealed to contemporary readers, since they occur together in three of the five incomplete manuscripts of *Eight Chapters*, while in a fourth, B. L. Add. MS 60577, chapter eight appears on its own (ed. Professor Takamiya, *Poetica* vol. xii, 1981).

Angels' Song is extant in six known manuscripts and one black-letter edition. For translation I have chosen the text of B. L. Add. MS 27592, edited by Professor Toshiyuki Takamiya, (*Studies in English Literature*, English Number 1977) and reprinted privately in 1980 with *Eight Chapters on Perfection*. Again, I am greatly indebted to Professor Takamiya for permission to make use of his work.

I would like to thank the Revd J. P. H. Clark, the author of an important series of articles on Hilton in *The Downside Review*, 1977-1979, for kindly reading my typescript and giving advice on the translation of theological terms; Professor Valerie Lagorio for suggesting this small project and encouraging its publication; Dame Helen Gardner for introducing me to Hilton studies many years ago; and Professor A. J. Bliss for helping me to return to them.

ROSEMARY DORWARD

INTRODUCTION

The fourteenth century, and in particular the second half of the fourteenth century, was a very special moment in the history of the English language and of English Christianity. In 1300 it was still uncertain whether the language of this country would be English or French. By 1400 it had become clear that English had triumphed. Not only that, but to the same period belong three poets of outstanding genius: Chaucer, Langland and the unknown author of *Sir Gawayne and the Green Knight*, men whose work continues to be a living part of the English literary heritage wherever the language is spoken and studied.

But the fourteenth century was not only a great moment for English poetry; it was also a great moment for English prose. These years saw the emergence of a group of mystical writers whose work, for depth and penetration, fervour and discernment, has never since been surpassed. Richard Rolle, the anonymous author of *The Cloud of Unknowing*, Julian of Norwich and Walter Hilton, the author of the two short treatises contained in this little book. And these writers too have proved to be very much alive in our late twentieth century. In the last decades, Julian's *Revelations of Divine Love* and *The Cloud of Unknowing*, to name only the two best known works of this period, have been more widely read than at any previous time. It seems in a strange way as though these writers of six centuries ago had been writing with our own time in view; for this reason alone it is a particular pleasure to be able to make them accessible in clear and accurate modern English.

Perhaps the relevance of these writers to our own situation need not be so surprising after all. In the first place they were writing about the deep things of the human spirit, and the deep things of the mystery of God, and the changes which sweep over the turbulent surface of our society scarcely influence these things. What they saw and declared can often speak directly to us. In the second place their own time had been far from undisturbed. It had seen natural disasters, the Black Death in the middle of the century and social and political unrest culminating in the Peasants' Revolt a generation later. Theirs, like ours was not an easy century in which to live. But it is also clear that they wrote in an age and in a society which gave greater attention to the things of the spirit than we do in ours, and thus we feel in their writing an assurance, a balance, a wisdom and a discernment which our own time often lacks.

It may be this quality of discernment and discretion (the two words are closely linked) which strikes us first in the two treatises presented here. 'See', writes Walter Hilton, 'I have told you a little about this subject as it appears to me, not claiming that this is enough, or that it is the truth of the matter. If it seems otherwise to you, or if any other man experience the contrary by grace, discard what I have said and give preference to him.' Here is a man very far removed from fanaticism or rigidity, with no inflated sense of the importance of his own perception of things. But the same man who is prepared to be so tentative in his judgement on the growth of the inner life, can be absolutely clear and definite in his affirmation of the common articles of the faith. 'Be sure that the supreme end of perfection consists in the true union of God with man's soul through perfect charity.' There are areas where one feels one's way, explores and speculates. There are boundaries given which are axiomatic, certain.

This distinction between our common faith in the mystery of God, and the varying ways in which people come to experience it in their own lives is fundamental to the understanding of these treatises. Both are concerned with the place where faith and experience meet, where the action of grace sets in motion in man's heart and mind intuitions, feelings, perceptions, which are not always easy to understand or to control. The writer is concerned to distinguish between the action of God within us and our experience of that action. This distinction, which is not always a simple one, is vital to growth in the spiritual life as well as to growth in human sanity and wholeness. It is easy to mistake our own feelings for the action of God's Spirit, our own experience of grace for the mysterious reality of grace itself. Whenever people are deeply stirred by God's action within them, as they are in the twentieth century no less than in the fourteenth, these questions are bound to arise and need to be clarified.

It is indeed the case that a number of movements in the last ten or fifteen years—some more outwardly expressive and 'charismatic', some more inward and contemplative—which have led people into new and unexpected experiences of prayer, make these two little treatises surprisingly relevant. At first sight, a discussion of angels' song or a series of warnings about possible dangers in relationships between men and women vowed to celibacy, might seem rather remote from our concerns. But it is very clear that when the Spirit of God stirs in the heart of man, levels of human awareness are opened up—psychic, intuitive, 'angelic'—which can resound in curious and sometimes fascinating ways. Similarly, when human hearts are deeply moved by God's love, it is easy enough to mistake for the operations of that love various more human forms of loving which may or may not be wrong in themselves, but which certainly need to be seen for what they are.

So in the treatise on *Angels' Song*, Hilton makes a number of very careful and fine distinctions between various kinds of inner exaltation which may be experienced in the life of prayer. He does not deny that a soul made perfect in love may experience such a heavenly music; he sees it as a sign that the whole of man's nature, bodily as well as spiritual, can be caught up into the transforming action of God's grace. But he is also aware that those who have not advanced so far towards union with God may be deceived, may imagine that they hear and perceive heavenly sounds, when in fact all that is stirred within them is their own imagination. And then he allows for a third condition, somewhere between the other two, in which a person's heart may be filled with a sense of song, a kind of music, after he has been practising, for instance, some form of the Jesus prayer. But this Hilton declares 'is not angels' song, but a song of the soul, in the strength of the Name and by the touch of the good angel'. Here evidently is a man with much experience in these matters, one whose judgement we feel instinctively we may trust, especially when he concludes, after this careful analysis of different kinds of feeling, 'It is enough for me to live principally in faith, and not in feeling.'

The *Eight Chapters on Perfection* breathe a similar discernment and moderation. We are not to allow ourselves to be turned aside from prayer by the fact that we sometimes meet with times of darkness and aridity. We are to persevere on our way, but with discretion and good sense, not forcing ourselves immoderately. Similarly, we are to be wary of those who speak much of their experiences or who who claim to have reached a liberty in the Spirit which emancipates them from all common claims of God's law. Above all we are to be wary of the way in which a truly spiritual love between a man and a woman may gradually turn into a predominantly fleshly and human affection. At first sight, Hilton's teaching at this point may seem entirely negative. He deals with the question in chapter five and comes back to it in greater detail, much of it very finely observed, in chapter eight. He was evidently speaking of situations which were familiar to him, about which he felt deeply.

Two things are to be observed. First, we may assume that he is speaking here about relationships between persons vowed to celibacy, to whom the option of marriage is not open. Secondly, though he is very insistent on the possibilites of delusion and danger in such relationships of deeper spiritual friendship, he never seems to exclude them totally. Indeed he seems to assume that loving relationships between persons vowed to celibacy or, we might suppose, between married people and those other than their spouses, *should* be possible when once they have received the grace of discretion. Then a man or woman 'will know from experience whose company and intercourse he should escape as harmful and without profit, and whose company and affection he should covet for the ease and support they give him.' Just as in the other treatise there is no suggestion that we should try to ignore or suppress our feelings, though we shall seek to live principally in truth and not in feeling, so here there is no suggestion that because we ought to be acutely aware of the possibilities of self-deception in matters of the heart, we should therefore seek to stifle our affections or aim at some condition of insensibility where we should no longer need the joy and support which our friends can give us.

Throughout these pages there breathes a spirit which combines light with warmth, fervour with discretion. It is the same spirit which we find, in different forms, in the writings of Julian and in *The Cloud of Unknowing*. It is a spirit which speaks of the way in which, when we turn from all things to God, putting his will and his glory before all else, then we find that creation is given back to us, full of his goodness. 'This is the freedom and lordship and nobility and honour that a man's soul has above all created beings, and this nobility he can recover here by grace, so that he perceives every created thing as it is; and that is when by grace he sees, hears and feels only God in all creatures.'

Feast of the Annunciation 1983   A. M. ALLCHIN

EIGHT CHAPTERS ON PERFECTION

This is the beginning of eight chapters necessary for men who devote themselves to becoming perfect. They were found in a book by Master Lluis de Font[1] at Cambridge and translated into English by Master Walter Hilton of Thurgarton.

I
The signs and operations of love.

II
What to do when devotion is withdrawn.

III
The dangers that a spiritual man has to avoid.

IV
The degrees by which a soul progresses
to contemplation.

V
The dangers of spiritual love.

VI
The perfect love of Christ, without which
all other love is suspect.

VII
The transformation of the soul into love of Jesus Christ.

VIII
How spiritual love often turns into carnal love.

---

1. MS Lowis de Fontibus.

I

The signs and operations of love.

The first sign of love is the lover's complete submission of his own will to the will of the beloved; and this special kind of love works in three ways.

In the first, if the beloved is simple and poor, humble and despised, then his lover longs to be like him: wretched, poor, meek and in disgrace.

The second compels a man to leave every kind of affection or friendship that runs contrary to this love; so it makes him forsake his father and all other affections in so far as they cross the will of the beloved.

Thirdly, there is nothing hidden in his heart that he will not show to the other: this is a particular sign of deep love between two people, and in this are fulfilled the operations already described, because through this revealing of secrets their hearts are opened and they are the more perfectly bound together.

II

What to do when devotion is withdrawn.

If you want to ascend continually towards perfection and to persevere in the way of God which you have entered, you must go on making more and more progress and growing from virtue to virtue. When the grace of devotion is withdrawn and you undergo temptations and great troubles you must pray no less than when you have grace without temptation.

But this is most acceptable and pleasing to God: when you are in great trouble and distress because your feeling of devotion is withdrawn, and yet nevertheless you pray, watch and do every other good deed; so continue the same good work on your own without devotion as you did before when you felt it. For this reason, if you sometimes meet those temptations and troubles that are ordained for the punishment and purifying of God's children, and devotion is withdrawn, brace yourself against any relaxation of prayer, watching or fasting, and stand no less firm in other good works. In this way, let your perseverance in prayer and in the tears of your eyes never cease until you as it were compel God to give you the fervour and heat of holy devotion.

Anyone who wants to be perfect and live according to this chapter should do as Cato says: 'Since you are living righteously, pay no attention to slander.'[1] Keep to your duty, and your dear beloved Jesus Christ will certainly do his part.

Prayer made with great effort, when the dull flesh would rather be lazy, is acceptable to God. It drives the beloved Jesus Christ to yield and to add to you grace and devotion, and great profit in temptation.

Therefore pray continually if you want to gain the grace of devotion for yourself and to make progress in the way of Christ. And whatever troubles and temptations you may meet, never stop praying, either as you carry on your business in the world, or in bed or out of bed, with other people or alone; for if you are in trouble or temptation and persevere in prayer, grace and devotion shall be added: Jesus Christ your beloved will himself give you new comfort. The devil may put the idea in your heart that your prayer is worthless, but despise and defy him in word and thought, and go on praying. The greater your trouble and affliction, the greater will be your comfort when the grace of devotion is given, so pray continually and read the book of life: that is the life of Jesus Christ, which consisted of poverty, humility, sorrow, scorn, grievous pain and faithful obedience. And when you have really started on this road, you will be troubled in various ways by many temptations and tribulations of the devil, the world and the flesh which will vastly torment and distress you; but if you want to overcome them all, pray resolutely and wait with patience for your beloved Jesus Christ: he will send you such indescribable help and relief that no tongue can tell its greatness.

When you are tortured with trouble or temptation, make

---

1. *Miss D. Jones traced this quotation to* liber III.2 *of* The Distichs of Cato, *a collection of moral sayings made by an unknown writer of the 2nd or 3rd century A.D.*

frequent use of confession as well as prayer: in this you will show your confessor, with full contrition of your heart, completely and honestly, all the wounds of your conscience, great and small, as extensively as you would show them to your own angel. This is a sovereign medicine for getting rid of temptations and troubles and obtaining the great grace of God's comfort, because the devil (being full of pride) cannot bear the meekness of pure confession, nor the fervour of perpetual prayer. Through these actions above all our sweet Lord Jesus Christ is drawn as if by violence into a loving soul and thus compelled to comfort it. Therefore concentrate all your desires and activities on preparing a place and a secret chamber in your soul for your Lord Jesus Christ, your husband,[1] by sweet meditation, by continual prayer, and by frequent confessions—made every day or every third day if one has the opportunity—so that the slightest hour of your time may not be forgotten in which you have in many things offended your honourable Lord and beloved Jesus Christ. Through these three activities—meditation, prayer and confession—many people come to the peace of a clean conscience. Be careful, however, that through negligence you give no foothold to the enemies that continually besiege you, which is what you do whenever you leave your prayers for some worthless or trivial occupation.

Therefore the more you are tempted and troubled, the more firmly dwell in prayer, and do not willingly interrupt it—except for weakness of the head or of your brain, as may sometimes happen through immoderate persistence in prayer or in watching or excessive fasting. Then it is good to stop for a while. Saint Jerome says: 'A man goes badly astray—not just slightly—if he prefers the lesser to the greater good': like somebody who values fasting more highly than helping others,[2] or who thinks the denial of sleep more important than holiness of brain, of sense and of reason. It is also a great mistake when a man by immoderate and ill-judged saying or singing of psalms or hymns falls into a frenzy or madness, or into the bitterness of depression. It is good, then, to check the multitude of words and just to think in your heart as easily as you can: and so through

---

1. MS spouse.　　　　　　　2. MS deedes of charite.

continual prayer, in mouth or in heart, you shall be set free and relieved of your temptations.

By persevering in prayer a soul is given the light of grace, which clears the conscience and lays its foundations in a deep and genuine humility. And through continually consulting and reading the book of life—that is, the blessed person Jesus Christ and his life—the soul is rooted and grounded in patience and in love,[1] since the study of that book can instruct and train you in all you need to know. By this means you shall acquire such patience that you will want to welcome every kind of trouble and hardship as a great support, since by them you shall feel and see yourself as a little like your Lord Jesus Christ whom you love. Yes, you shall regard yourself as so unwise and so unworthy in God's sight that it will be no hardship to bear whatever you have to suffer, because beyond comparison he suffered more for you. Nevertheless, you shall still trust and hope that as you are his comrade in pain and hardship—slight though they may be—so you shall be with him in his joy and bliss, for as the Apostle says: 'If we are sharers of Christ's sufferings, we shall be sharers of his blessed consolations.'[2]

It therefore seems that a man can attain no greater dignity or worth than to bear tribulation for the love of Christ, by which he becomes Christ's comrade here in this life and in the bliss of heaven for ever. Amen.

III

The dangers that a spiritual man has to avoid.

Be careful first not to give yourself, nor your whole affection, nor your intimate friendship to anyone unless you have already received the gift and the spirit of discretion by which you may know whom to avoid and whom to approach. Until you achieve this, be straightforward and friendly while remaining a little aloof from everyone—always excepting the duty of Christian kindness.[3] Also, be particularly wary of people who talk charmingly and

1. MS charite.   2. 2 Cor. 1.5   3. MS charite

have no holiness in terms of virtue nor sweetness of heart, but only a likeness of holiness in their speech and bearing: those who show off, boasting of visions, revelations, unusual feelings, singular actions or insights,[1] or understandings higher than other men's, through which they are admired and receive exaggerated praise and honour from those they speak to. Such people are often deceitful snares for the unwise. First consider them, look at them, and bring them in your mind to the presence of Jesus Christ—exactly as if you wanted to take something out of a dark place to find out what it was—and set it down and look at it in the light. Just so, Jesus Christ is light, and there is no light of grace or of truth except Christ himself and the light that is in him. Therefore bring men of this kind and of every other—yes, and yourself with them—to Jesus Christ, in your prayers and in your mind. There they shall be seen as they are; there they shall be tried; and there through gazing at him and his life you shall see who is like him and who unlike. However, be careful not to judge a man completely by your view of him, for all things are uncertain in the secret judgement of God. Still, by this reference to Christ's life you may follow and direct your own conscience on this point: whom you shall follow and whom refuse; with whom you can be familiar and with whom you must be reserved. That kind of judgement is necessary to you.

Be careful too about fervours. For example, if you begin to feel an intense excitement of the spirit,[2] think first and consider well before you follow its action through: how it has begun and what has caused it; its course and its result. Then follow it as far as you can understand by grace and counsel, and by Holy Scripture: that is, according to the true virtue of discretion and to the life of Christ. You shall make that life your mirror, your rule, and the example that you follow: for this reason observe the inward quality of Christ more than its outward expression in his teaching.

Yet again, beware of people who claim to have won the spirit of freedom, saying they have so much grace by love that they may live as they please. They think themselves so free and so

---

1. MS wittes   2. MS if thou feele the sperit of feruour gretli fallen vpon thee

secure that they shall not sin. They set themselves above the law of Holy Church, and cite St Paul: 'Where the Spirit of God is, there is freedom.'[1] And so too: 'If you are led by the Spirit, you are not under the Law.'[2] But their meaning is not Paul's; they do not understand his words. These men are expressly against the life of Christ. The reason is that Christ who was made free made himself a slave for us; and when he was above the Law as maker and giver of it, he yet made himself obedient under the Law.[3] St Peter speaks thus of these men: 'They promise others freedom of spirit, and they themselves are slaves in sin and servants of fleshly corruption.'[4]

IV

The degrees by which a soul progresses to contemplation.

The first degree is in tears, and in sighing and sorrow for sins; in contrition and compassion for the suffering of Christ; and in sympathy for the distress and misery of one's fellow Christian. There is great effort against every kind of vice—evil deeds, words, intentions and thoughts—all of which are opposed with great trouble and painful labour of body and soul.

The second degree is great fervour and burning desire—with continuing prayer—to please Jesus Christ, to love him with all your heart and all your strength, and to feel the comfort of his gracious presence. This burning desire will cleanse the conscience from all the rust of sin, both that already committed and what one falls into day by day. This work is done with great effort and wonderful diligence, a little tempered and interspersed with rest.

The third degree is a state of wonderful sweetness and softness, of joy, of rest and of clarity; for here the grace of the Holy Spirit descends into a soul. Then it makes the soul so bright and pure [that it is all like (an) eye; and it anoints the soul][5] with the oil of spiritual gladness and turns it all into love[6]

1. 2 Cor. 3.17   2. Gal. 5.18   3. Phil. 2.5-8
4. 2 Pet. 2.19   5. *Supplied from other MSS.*   6. MS charite

7

of Christ, so that it feels all the limbs of the body and all the structure of the world, with every created thing, to be like a melody on the harp. Then after this the soul is in some degree fit for the spiritual embraces of Jesus Christ, her sweet husband.[1]

The fourth degree exists in supreme rest of body and soul. That is when a man is dead and buried to the world and the flesh, reposing in peace of conscience, and rests[2] ever continually in our Lord Jesus Christ without the disturbance[3] of vain thoughts.

The fifth degree is when a man begins to accept in faith the pledge of endless joy and is lifted up to gaze at heavenly things. Then he feels and perceives a glimmer of heavenly bliss, and sees something of the state of angels and blessed souls, realizing how all illuminations and all the graces of charity and goodness descend out of the Trinity—blessed beyond description—into the man Jesus Christ; and how from that glorious manhood of Christ all the graces of light and love stream forth into angels and into holy souls, and from them come down to us. And then a man is made able to receive the revelations of Jesus Christ, and to contemplate him.

V

The dangers of holy love.

A man of exalted reputation was often asked to speak about spiritual love, and then he would recount the falsehood, perils and deceits that often attend it, saying: 'There is nothing in the whole world—man, devil or anything else—that I mistrust so strongly as the affection of love, or anything that I fear so much, unless it is wisely placed. The reason is that love is such an extreme thing and holds so fast that it sinks deeper in the soul than anything else. Nothing so completely occupies and binds and overpowers a man's heart as does love in its fullness, whether it be good love or bad. Therefore unless a man or woman is

1. MS spouse   2. *or* rises: *the manuscripts disagree.*
3. *or* struggling *(most other MSS, with various forms).*

armed with discretion by which to hold and rule love, it will easily overthrow the soul and bring it shamefully to the ground. I am not speaking of the carnal love that is obviously wrong—which should be hated by all Christ's lovers as a thing most devilish, most dangerous and most contrary to the chastity of Christ's love—but I speak of good spiritual love that is and ought to be between God and man, man and man, and man and woman. For this reason: the love that a soul has conceived through the grace of Jesus Christ must be established and ruled with great humility and discretion, and its fervour controlled by reason, certainly; otherwise it does not last but soon fails and vanishes away, or else it makes a man begin some projects with so much enthusiasm that he cannot persevere and so wants to escape from them.

'Moreover the love between man and man, and man and woman—as between devout men and devout women—that is in God and set for God, should be very carefully watched, and controlled with the weapons of discretion: otherwise it turns into carnal love and lechery, or else it causes great loss and waste of time through empty talk and conversation together, because their hearts are unwisely fastened in love. This often happens to people—whether men or women—that love each other, but it is most especially dangerous when a man and woman love each other with as good intentions as they can themselves discern. They love each other heartily in such a good and virtuous manner that it seems they would never willingly part; and they have a great and singular mutual affection because of the goodness that one sees in the other, making each of them help and comfort the other in many ways. And what they do for each other is all for the love of their hearts. Yes, too much from the heart! For it seems to them that they would like always to be together. Whatever one likes pleases the other, and what displeases one is disliked by the other. This love is very dangerous and entirely to be blamed—although it seems good—and it is the more dangerous in that its danger is not recognized: for it will all turn to lust unless it is ruled and controlled with the armoury of discretion.'

VI

The perfect love of Christ, without which all other love is suspect.

The best and truest love is when a soul is lifted and illuminated into the knowledge of the Being of God in Christ—as when the soul sees how each creature receives its being from him who is supreme Being, that is, God—and it sees that nothing has true being but God.

From this knowledge the soul receives a wonderful pleasure, with a great understanding that whatever derives from that supreme Being is good, and that all that he does is excellent. This knowledge stirs and arouses a love in the soul, responding to that spiritual gazing upon the Being of Christ. This knowledge also makes a man love all that takes its being from him—that is, every creature, whether rational or irrational—for love of him that gives being to all creation. Especially it moves the soul to love those creatures that have reason, and most of all those which it perceives to be most loved by Christ; for as the soul sees Jesus Christ inclined to the love of all creatures, so it is itself inclined. Then the soul is taught to love creatures more or less according to the measure and quality of Christ's love for them and their love for him; and the grace of Christ in this way keeps the soul from excess. Therefore until you feel this kind of love (derived from the spiritual knowledge of Christ's Being) firmly founded in your heart, regard all your love with suspicion, and be afraid.

But when you can reach the point of steadying the sight of your soul on this blessed person Jesus Christ and on his supreme Being—in weal and in woe, in ease and in distress—without much turning your gaze away from him: then the wonderful love that results from this knowledge and this gazing is enough to guard you against the venomous darts of all carnal loves, and to drive out their malice from the attention[1] of the soul.

1. MS mynde

VII

The transformation of the soul into the love of Jesus Christ.

There are three ways in which the soul may be transformed.

One is for the soul to be made humble and obedient to the will of God, so that it sets itself to resemble him in every possible way, following his actions, and to transfigure and turn and hold in itself Christ's Passion, bearing every shame and rebuke as he did, so that it would rather be like Christ through suffering distress than enjoy all the entertainment in the world.

There is a second way to be transformed with God, and that is when one's soul is united with Christ and becomes his familiar friend. The soul then has a great awareness of Christ's love, and often receives the hidden sweetness of his inspiration and many great comforts and delights: yet they are not too great to be expressed in thought and word.

The third kind of transformation is when Jesus Christ and a soul are so perfectly, inseparably and harmoniously united and bound together that Christ is in the soul and the soul is in him as fully as if both were a single spirit, as Saint Paul says: 'Whoever holds fast to God is one spirit with him.'[1] Then the soul experiences high mysteries of Jesus Christ and of his Father and of the Holy Spirit, and it receives such joys from Christ's charity as cannot be fully realized by human thought or expressed in the words of human language.

The first transformation is not enough to rule and govern the affection of man's heart, and neither is the second. The reason is that the fervour of affection, whether its activity is aimed at God or man, is often mightier, fiercer and more dominant than the wise discretion of the soul; and therefore while it is so the love may slip and stumble and err, through being too great or too little.

By the third, however, wisdom and deep knowledge are secretly poured into the soul through that wonderful mingling

1. 1 Cor. 6.17

and union of Christ's shining light with the soul that receives it, so that the soul is taught by the spirit of discretion how to be ruled, and how to govern the love that it has in Christ. It will be taught to receive spiritual feelings and hidden sweetness and joys in Christ, and how to order, rule and control the fervours of Christ's love and the visits of his gracious presence so wisely, so secretly and so soberly that it can go on experiencing the spiritual comforts of Christ's love quite easily, without revealing itself in the sight of others by laughing or sobbing, or any eccentricity of behaviour.

Moreover, by the same spirit of discretion the soul is shown how wisely, soberly, chastely, meekly and lovingly it shall behave towards fellow-Christians—men and women—and how gladly and graciously to come down to them when it sees that the time, the person and the cause are opportune. And when he sees that such condescension is unwise he will not stoop to them in any way, but keeps remarkably stiff, unbending and strong, like some object that cannot be moved, changed or bowed at all.

The reason is this. God is changeless in himself, but a soul is by nature changeable. When the soul is made one with Christ by love, the more closely it is united the more unchangeable it is, and the less changeability it has, because the wisdom and knowledge, the stability and the light of discretion that the soul has through this union in love gives it love and power: weapons with which it can rule the affection of love for God and for its fellow-Christian without error or deceit. So for a man who has never felt these gifts of discretion, wisdom and grace in his heart it is expedient not to let his affection be completely tied to any creature—man or woman—either individually, secretly or to excess, because of the dangers that may easily result; but let him be frank and open with all and not intimate with any, until he can by this light of discretion know from experience whose company and intercourse he should avoid as harmful and without profit, and whose company and affection he should covet for the ease and support they give him.

VIII

How spiritual love is turned into carnal love.

It often happens that a devout man loves another devout man, or a devout woman, with good honourable love and with a good will in the sight of God. Later this love increases so much between them that each has an immoderate longing for the other's company, to the point where they grow depressed and sick if they cannot be together at will. Sometimes when they meet their affection continues to grow, so that they are even more lovesick, and this binds their hearts in such close intimacy that what one wants the other wants too, and whatever pleases or displeases one pleases or displeases the other, whether it be good or evil. It is very dangerous for a man and woman to be thus deeply wounded with the affection of love, for it is when their hearts agree so familiarly that they need to express the heart's meaning sometimes, by further tokens that do not seem very wrong. So by words and signs, as they show each other how much they love, their love is more enlarged and further changed from spiritual to carnal; but still they are eager to disguise and hide the carnal affection under the purity of Christian love,[1] of spiritual progress and of building up the soul, for they tell each other that they intend nothing but good. So, in the security of that intention and of that false assumption, each longs to touch and feel and kiss the other, regarding it as devotion and good love when really it is lecherous love and the slaying of devotion: a great hindrance and harm to the soul that wants and ought to feel the love of Christ.

Nevertheless at first their reason does grumble a little against it, and their conscience is often in revolt, for the reason is not yet completely strangled and slain through habitual contact. When such behaviour does become a habit, reason is blinded and strangled and the conscience falsely lulled, so that they feel there is no danger for them in using such words and looks,

1. MS charite

13

touches of hand and body, kissing and similar tokens of fleshly love. Sometimes they say that they may do this, and though it may be a sin, yet it is nothing much: and so, ever little by little, spiritual love declines and dies and carnal love grows and flourishes. After this, as time goes on, the fervour of love increases so much that it takes away their tongues and all the powers of their souls, to such a degree that neither will refuse the other for fear of giving displeasure in anything that either wants to do—even though it were mortal sin. When it has gone so far, neither talking nor touching, fondling, kissing nor physical presence can wholly satisfy their love, and then they are impassioned by the temptation of the devil to agree upon the act of fornication, and to complete it if opportunity arises.

Because this danger may easily occur through the mismanagement of love, it is good for you to regard with suspicion and dread every kind of love in yourself when it is secretly and individually fixed on any one person, man or woman. Although it may be good and spiritual at first, beginning in God and goodness, it often becomes evil and carnal later on, and ends in the works of the devil.

From such love and its perils may all of us Christians be saved in the way shown above, by the weapons of discretion gained through the wounds of Christ. Amen.

ANGELS' SONG

by

Walter Hilton

Dear brother in Christ, I understand from your own words and also by someone else's report that you are longing for more knowledge and guidance about the song of angels and heavenly sound: what it is, and in what way it is perceived and felt in a man's soul; how one may be sure that it is genuine and not a delusion; and how it is made by the presence of the good angel and not put into the soul by the bad. This you want to learn of me, but in fact I cannot tell you the certain truth of the matter; however, I shall briefly show you something as it seems to me.

Be sure that the supreme end of perfection consists in a true union of God with man's soul through perfect charity. This union is truly made when the powers of the soul are reformed by grace to the honourable state of its first condition: that is, when the mind is established firmly, without change or straying, in God and spiritual things; when the reason is cleared of all worldly and carnal sights, and from all bodily imaginations, symbols and fantasies of things created, and is illuminated by grace to behold God and spiritual things; and when the will and the affection are purged and cleansed from all fleshly, natural and worldly love and are set on fire with burning love by the Holy Ghost.

This wonderful union cannot be achieved perfectly, continually and completely in this life because of the corrupting influence of the flesh, but only in the bliss of heaven. Nevertheless, the nearer that a soul can come to such union in this present life, the more perfect it is; for the more that it is thus reformed by grace here to the image and likeness of its creator, the more joy and bliss it shall have in heaven. Our Lord is an endless Being without change, omnipotence without failure; supreme wisdom, light and truth without error or darkness; supreme goodness, love, peace and sweetness. Then the more that a soul is united, fastened, conformed and joined to him, the more stable and powerful it is; the more wise and clear, good and peaceable, loving and virtuous it is; and so it is more perfect. A soul is made as perfect as is possible in this life when it has by the grace of Jesus and long labour of bodily and spiritual exercise overcome and destroyed gross desires,[1] passions and irrational impulses within itself, as well as without in the animal nature,[2] and is clothed completely in virtues: for example, in meekness and mildness; in patience and tenderness; in spiritual strength and righteousness; in self-control and wisdom; in faith, hope and love.[3] It receives great comfort from our Lord: not only within, in its own hidden substance, by virtue of the union with our Lord that consists in knowledge and love of God, in his light and spiritual incandescence, in the transforming of the soul in the Godhead—but also many other comforts, savours, sweetnesses, and wonderful feelings in various ways, as our Lord vouchsafes to visit his creatures here on earth, and as the soul advances and grows in love.[4]

A certain soul may be so purified through the power of the love[5] bestowed on it by God that all created things and all that he hears, sees or feels by any of his senses turns him to comfort and joy, and the animal nature finds fresh savour and sweetness in everything that is made. Just as the pleasures of the sensual nature were formerly carnal, vain and vicious as punishment for original sin, so now they are made spiritual and pure, without bitterness or biting of conscience. This is the goodness of our Lord, that—since the soul is punished in the sensual nature and the flesh is its partner in pain—afterwards the soul should be refreshed through the senses, and the body made the soul's companion in comfort and joy—not carnal but spiritual—even as they were comrades in affliction and pain. This is the freedom and lordship, nobility and honour that a man's soul has above all created things, and this nobility he can recover here by grace, so that he relishes every created thing as it is: and that is when by grace he sees, hears and feels only God in all creatures. In this way a soul is made spiritual even in its sensual nature through the abundant charity that exists in the substance of the soul.

1. MS concupiscens   2. MS sensualite *is represented variously by*
3., 4., 5. MS charite   animal nature, sensual nature *and* senses.

Our Lord also comforts a soul by angels' song. What that song is may not be described through any physical comparison, for it is spiritual and above any kind of imagination or reason. It can be felt and perceived in a soul, but it cannot be demonstrated. Nevertheless I tell you about it as it seems to me.

When a soul is purified by the love of God, illuminated by wisdom and made steadfast by God's power, its eye is opened to gaze at spiritual things, and virtues, angels, holy souls and the things of heaven. Then because of its purity the soul is able to sense the touching and speaking of good angels. This touching and speaking is spiritual, not bodily: when the soul is raised and caught up[1] out of the animal nature and away from the thought of any earthly things it is in a great glow of feeling[2] by the love and light of God, and if our Lord grants it the soul may hear and feel heavenly sound, made by the company of angels praising God. Not that this song of angels is the supreme joy of the soul: but because of the difference that exists through impurity between a man's embodied soul and an angel, a soul may not hear it except by being caught up in love and needs to be completely purified and filled with great charity before it is able to hear heavenly sound. For the supreme and essential joy lies in the love of God by himself and for himself, and the joy of seeing and communicating with angels and spiritual creatures is secondary. Just as a soul is often touched and taught to understand spiritual things through bodily imagination by the work of angels (as Ezekiel the prophet saw the truth of God's mysteries in bodily imagination), so in the love of God a soul through the presence of angels is caught up from the thought of all earthly and carnal things into a heavenly joy, to hear angels' song and heavenly sound according to the measure of its charity.

Now it seems to me that no soul may truly sense the song of angels or heavenly sound unless he is in perfect charity. Nevertheless not everyone in perfect charity has felt it, but only the soul so refined in the fire of love that every earthly pleasure is burnt out of it, and every hindrance between the soul and the cleanness of angels is broken and put away. Then indeed may he sing a new song and truly hear a joyful heavenly sound and song

---

1. MS rauisched   2. MS feruour

of angels, without falsehood or pretence. Our Lord knows where that soul is whose abundance of burning love makes it worthy to hear angels' song. Therefore, whoever wants to hear angels' song, undeceived by pretence or his own imagination or by the trickery of the enemy, must have perfect charity: and that is when all vain love and dread, vain joy and sorrow are cast out of the heart, so that he loves nothing but God, dreads nothing but God, and rejoices or mourns over nothing except in God or for God. Whoever by God's grace takes this path should not go astray.

Nevertheless, some men are deceived in this matter by their own imagination or by the trick of the enemy. Someone who has toiled for a long time in body and spirit to destroy sins and acquire virtues, and who has perhaps by grace obtained a little rest and a clear conscience, at once stops praying, reading Holy Scripture, meditating on the passion of Christ and considering his own wretchedness: before being called by God he violently gathers his wits together to seek out and gaze upon heavenly things with an eye not yet made spiritual by grace; he over-strains his wits with imagination, and with immoderate effort turns the brains in his head, shattering the powers and faculties of the soul and body; then through the weakness of his brain he seems to hear wonderful sounds and songs, yet it is nothing but a fantasy caused by confusion of the brain. Like a man in a frenzy, it seems to him that he hears and sees what nobody else does, but it is all just an idle fantasy in his head, or else it comes through the work of the enemy who contrives such a sound in his hearing.

For if a man entertains any presumption in his fancies and his exercises by which he slips into uncontrolled imagination—into a frenzy, as it were—and is not instructed or ruled by grace or sustained by spiritual strength, the devil enters his soul by means of false illuminations, false sounds and sweetness, and deceives it. From this false ground spring errors and heresies, false pro-phecies, presumptions, false ravings, blasphemies and slanders, and many other evils. Therefore, if you see any man of spiritual occupation fall into any of these sins and deceits or into fits of frenzy, be sure that he never heard or sensed the song of angels or heavenly sound; for indeed someone who truly hears angels' song is made so wise that he will never go astray through fantasy, or by indiscretion, or by any contrivance of the devil.

Also, some men feel in their hearts in various ways something like a spiritual sound and sweet singing: this is usually good, though sometimes it may turn into deceit. Such a sound is perceived like this: some man sets the thought of his heart only on the name of Jesus and steadfastly holds it there. In a short time that name seems to turn to great comfort and sweetness for him, and he feels it sounding delightfully in his heart like a song, and the force of this pleasure is so strong that it draws into itself all the senses of the soul. Whoever can feel this sound and this sweetness genuinely in his heart may be sure that is from God, and as long as he is humble he shall not be deceived. However, this is not angels' song but a song of the soul, in the strength of the name and by the touch of the good angel; for when a soul offers itself truly and humbly to Jesus, putting all its trust and desire in him and keeping him intently in mind, our Lord Jesus, when he wishes, purges the affection of the soul; he fills and feeds it with his own sweetness and makes his name like honey in the soul's perception, and like song, and like anything that gives delight. So it pleases the soul to cry, 'Jesu, Jesu, Jesu' continually; and it has comfort not only in this but also in the psalms, hymns and anthems of Holy Church, causing the heart to sing them sweetly, devoutly and freely, without any effort or distress of the soul, to the same time and notes that Holy Church uses. This is good and by God's gift, for the substance of this feeling consists in the love of Jesus, which is fed and illuminated by song of this kind. Nevertheless, in this kind of feeling a soul may be deceived by vainglory: not at the time when the affection sings to Jesus and loves him in his sweetness, but later when it ceases and the heart's love for Jesus cools; then it passes into vainglory.

Again, a man may be deceived in this way: he hears it rightly said that it is good to keep 'Jesus' in his mind—or any other good word of God—and then he forces his heart powerfully towards that name, and from habit has it nearly always in his thought; not that he feels through it any sweetness in his affection or light of knowledge in his reason, but just the naked thought of 'God', 'Jesus', 'Mary', or any other good word. He

19

may be deceived: not because it is wrong to keep Jesus in mind like this, but if he regards this feeling and this attention (which is only his own habitual exercise) as a special visitation from our Lord, and thinks it more than it is. For you must know that a naked thought or imagining of Jesus or any spiritual thing, without sweetness of love in the affection or light of knowledge in the reason, is only a blindness and a way to deceit if a man overvalues it in his own sight. Therefore I hold it certain that he should be humble in his own feeling and set no value on this thought until he can by habitual use of it feel the fire of love in his affection and the light of knowing in his reason.

See, I have told you a little about this subject as it appears to me, not claiming that this is enough, or that it is the truth of the matter. If it seems otherwise to you, or if any other man experiences the contrary by grace, discard what I have said and give preference to him. It is enough for me to live principally in faith, and not in feeling.

SUGGESTIONS FOR FURTHER READING

I DISCUSSION AND REFERENCE

Helen L. Gardner. *Walter Hilton and the Mystical Tradition in England, Essays and Studies* xxii, 1936, pp. 103-127.

Phyllis Hodgson. *Three Fourteenth Century English Mystics*, London, 1967 (Bibliographical Series of Supplements to *British Book News* on *Writers and their Work*).

David Knowles. *The English Mystical Tradition*, London 1961.

James Walsh SJ (edited and introduced). *Pre-Reformation English Spirituality*, London 1966. This is a collection of articles reprinted from *The Month*, including an essay on Walter Hilton by J. Russell-Smith, p. 182-197.

Valerie M. Lagorio and Ritamary Bradley. *The 14th Century English Mystics: A Comprehensive Annotated Bibliography*, Garland Publishing, New York and London, 1981.

II EDITIONS

The Minor Works of Walter Hilton, edited by Dorothy Jones, Orchard Books xvii, London, 1929. It contains *Mixed Life, Eight Chapters on Perfection, Qui Habitat, Bonum Est* and *Benedictus*, all edited from Lambeth MS 472, with detailed notes and a valuable introduction. The spelling has been modernized, but otherwise this version is very close to the Middle English text.

The Goad of Love. An unpublished translation by Walter Hilton of the *Stimulus Amoris*, edited from manuscripts by Clare Kirchberger, Classics of the Contemplative Life, London, 1952. The editor's comparison of Hilton's text with the original Latin work by James of Milan is of great value to anyone wanting to study his methods of translation and assess his share in the substance of *Eight Chapters on Perfection.*

The Scale of Perfection, edited from MS sources with an introduction by Evelyn Underhill, London, 1923, reprinted 1948.

The Scale of Perfection, translated into modern English with an introduction and notes by Dom Gerard Sitwell OSB, Orchard Books, London, 1953.

The Ladder of Perfection. A new translation with an introduction by Leo Sherley-Price, Penguin Classics, London, 1957.

The Scale of Perfection. Text of Leo Sherley-Price abridged and presented by Illtyd Trethowan, Monk of Downside, London, 1975.

The Stairway of Perfection, translated with introduction by M. L. del Mastro, Doubleday Image Books, New York, 1979.